Charlie Peck's lush, straightforward storytelling nevertheless holds something back. There are secrets here, lyric disconnects, the ancient ache in everything. Which is to say, these observant poems ring true whether they are or not. I bet both, as all treasures are. Honest and surprising, edgy and tender, urgently meditative, even shocking at times: these poems, thus this poet. Proof: "When I went down to the woods that first day of winter/I found a car door against a tree trunk, the paint rubbed thin/from deer shedding their velvet..." This is how legends start. And go where? I had to find out.

—MARIANNE BORUCH

"*Loss is unavoidable,*" our speaker encounters on an ancient bottle of Vick's VapoRub, and from the very beginning Charlie Peck plunges us right into this loss. Into loneliness. Into the mind and vision of a contemporary, self-aware Prufrock who downs cases of Hamm's and gas station fried chicken to the soundtrack of Prince and the Seinfeld theme on loop. *World's Largest Ball of Paint* crosses from the expanse of midwestern cornfields to the storm-riddled south and everywhere, *everywhere*, these poems take us, we won't be shielded from a thing. Not hurricanes, not racoons bloating in the back alley, not the knives laid-off cooks roll up and take home. Peck knows something about kitchens, about the fierce drama on and off the line, but also about how, no matter the frenzied dinner rush, no matter having to prepare a co-worker's syringe, one must craft a meticulous mise-en-place. In one poem, the edge of a poisoned tuna can is a "fanged lip." In another, the speaker recognizes, in an amateur painting, the desire to "organize pain into something useful." Charlie Peck is certainly no amateur, but in *World's Largest Ball of Paint* this desire becomes nearly electric. You might get shocked. But trust me, you'll come right back, touch these brilliant poems again and again.

—COREY VAN LANDINGHAM

T0355860

World's Largest Ball of Paint is written by a man who has earned his living as a cook. Charlie Peck speaks of what he knows well, 'the smell / of pork fat & garlic leading the way to the steel noodle counter.' His poems feed us. They feed us hunger, want, loneliness, loss, addiction, violence, boredom, depravity, laughter, grief, joy. The menu is memory. Watch out. Eating this poetry can burn your tongue. Bite down. The words may bite you back, but they will fill your mouth completely. They talk back. This is a book like the best Gaeng Keow Wan, green Thai curry. It is habanero hot.

—DONALD PLATT

WORLD'S LARGEST BALL OF PAINT

WORLD'S LARGEST BALL OF PAINT

poems

CHARLIE PECK

BLACK LAWRENCE PRESS

Black Lawrence Press

Executive Editor: Diane Goettel
Cover Artwork: "A Comedy at the Cookout" by Jack Felice
Book Cover and Interior Design: Zoe Norvell

Copyright © Charlie Peck 2024

ISBN: 978-1-62557-073-4

Published 2024 by Black Lawrence Press.
Printed in the United States.

for Nancy and Dave

TABLE OF CONTENTS

A Small Sweetness   xiii

I.

The Peanut Barrel   1

First Cigarette   3

Noise   5

New Year's Eve   7

My Car Got Towed   9

Jim & Milt's Bar-B-Q   11

Dear Kate   13

I pull on wool socks and jeans, pack   15

Elegy with Gulf Coast Hurricane & Prince   17

II.

The Radio Show   21

Head-On   23

The Possum   25

An Open Letter to the Block Explaining the Misshapen Hedge Around
    My Lawn   27

Dear Kate   29

Barricades   31

Elegy with Parrot & Tom Petty   33

III.

Bird's Aphrodisiac Oyster Shack   39

After Forgetting to Go to the Grocery Store and the Argument that
   Followed   41

Self-Portrait   45

Dear Kate (Poem in Which the *Seinfeld* Theme Repeats on Endless
   Loop)   46

Uphill Drift   48

Poem with a Juggalo in Plain Sight   50

Note to the Homeowners from the Housesitter   52

Sweat   54

Blood   56

Post-Christmas   58

Elegy with Scat Porn & Michael Jackson   60

IV.

Orientation Material for a New Neighbor Renting the Upstairs Unit,
   513 Perrin Ave., Lafayette, IN   65

Dear Kate   67

Thanksgiving   70

Algebra of Pleasure   72

Table Scratch   74

Leaving Lafayette   77

Elegy with Rotting Pumpkin & Mick Jagger   79

World's Largest Ball of Paint   82

Acknowledgments   87

A SMALL SWEETNESS

I have to guess that he's dead by now,
the man who offered twenty dollars outside
Macon to bring him to the Florida border,
but before we punched Valdosta he clipped out
clutching only a coffee tin and a pair of slippers.
In the rearview he marched lop-legged against
the rain, and that's it. In the long alphabets
of memory there are no clean-cut ends,
just the fat bits we bite when parts truck
violently back: gasoline fumes in a toilet stall,
every hot crotch of summer '07, the pair of red
canvas shoes I wore daily as my arm dipped
in and out of a loud oven in the brick back
of a restaurant whose name is long gone,
but the key still sleeps in my glovebox.
When I was a boy, I thought my father spoke
with an accent, stumbling through those mid-day
liquor-loops. *Sex with you*, one woman said
to me as each foot slipped back into snow boots,
feels like charity. It is good some mornings
to feel tired, pressed between two breasts
as a small voice reads the paper, the day too cold
to consider, lazy garlic wandering the house.
It must help that at the core of hurt hides
some small sweetness, that when the chef burned
his hands working the grill, he told me to cook
him up a shot. So I wrapped the cord, sucked

the spoon, and dropped the plunger deep
into the red flowerbed spreading in his arm.
His drooped eyes were not mine so I felt no hate.
Once in high school my brother caught me
bed-bound with a girl, so she and I left, skipped
the six blocks to her house to meet the garage door
open, her father purpled and swollen,
swinging from rafters, a bloated windchime.
I think that rope must have been tight
as a belt you can't unclasp fast enough
in a heated hotel room to pull yourself out
and be consumed by a wet, wanting mouth.
I hated animals and knew it meant I was heartless.
I was quick with a chef's knife so people called me
romantic. But it's not a butcher's red pool
that guts me — it's the sister, who headphoned
and high lay on her bed as her dad swung,
a metronome under muted floorboards.

I.

THE PEANUT BARREL

We're on the patio of the Peanut Barrel in East Lansing,
      Kate and I, having a pitcher in the heat. I order
    a round of fries because I know they're Kate's favorite,
and when we ask for ketchup our server says, *Of course.*
      They don't call me the Boss of Sauce for nothing,
    and I just love that. During the flood in '09, I foraged

through four feet of shit in my grandmother's basement
      in search of what was salvageable. I found a bottle
    of Vick's VapoRub from the '50s and in the fine print
below cedarleaf oils and menthol was written, *Close tightly.*
      Loss is unavoidable. My mind spins thinking of T
    from fourth grade, whose name was really Josh,

and no matter how often he reminded us of that fact,
      we called him T until one day, ten years old,
    he swallowed every pill in his dad's medicine cabinet.
When I meet someone new, I now repeat their name
      until I can't forget. Sarah, who cold brews
    my coffee. Matt, who walks his basset hound

each morning at six. Not everyone is so lucky to smear
      their mark like dog slobber on a windowpane.
    When I worked insurance my clients had no names,
just case numbers assigned, and daily I'd receive blunt
      memos, *C38-1442: Deceased, close account,*
    and though it was my job, it felt wrong that death

was a three-word footnote. Like everyone, I think about dying
            nonstop: frying chicken thighs, pinching the buds
      from the basil on my porch, sitting in my new office
leafing through page after page. We've had sex on my desk
            twice this week, Kate and I, because sometimes that's all
      you can do. We drink two more pitchers, and then a fourth,

eat another heap of fries as the taillights on Grand River Ave.
            blur. *I'm happy tonight, and my life is okay.* I read
      that somewhere and it comes to me now. We stand to leave.
Kate mentions to the host that we loved our server,
            and the host says, *Oh thank you, who did you have?*
      and Kate says, *We don't know, we never caught her name.*

FIRST CIGARETTE

Paul said the belly was softer than he expected
when he drove the knife into it, the homeless man's
on 13th behind O'Conner's Pub. I think I rubbed

my gut as he showed me the rusty blade as proof,
but I said nothing, hoping he'd abandon the rocks
he'd been terrorizing squirrels with and sell me

a cigarette. Under that maple tree Paul sold
a lone Marlboro to eleven-year-old me
for five bucks because he could. This was the summer

before our neighborhood was gerrymandered
into two different junior highs. Before Paul's dad
began sending him to CVS to shoplift Sudafed.

I don't know why I never told anyone. I'd seen
the headline on TV: *Homeless Man Found Stabbed
in Omaha Alley.* I'd held the knife. But I entered

a pact that day between smoke and silence
and to speak would betray every Camel snuck
behind bleachers and alleys for the next seven years

until I could buy my own. I'm now ten months removed
from my last, but the smell still brings back the cough
and a searing pain in my chest. How Paul turned

and walked back to his house, left me turning
the unlit thing in my hand. How I took my loose
smoke behind the brick schoolhouse and dragged

that first gulp, then pressed the ember tip
into my gut because that punishment was mine.

NOISE

I once attended a stand-up show in Amsterdam,
     and not speaking a word of Dutch I just laughed
     along with the crowd, letting myself get caught
up with the noise. It's the logic of applause
     and food fights. I can't think about the bubonic
     plague without getting anxious. When I watch

Planet Earth, I root for both prey and predator.
     The border between humor and disgust blurs
     neatly so it's often hard to say. I was driving
home from the grocery store last week
     and saw that my neighbor had painted and hung
     a new sign on his shed: THEEVES WILL BE SHOT

and Kate asked, *Who's Theeves?* In high school
     a boy did a Gallagher impression after prom,
     smashing watermelons on stage with a hammer,
his fake mustache falling off mid-swing,
     and then two weeks later his parents received a bill
     for $30,000 to replace the pulp-smattered curtain.

Or that time in second grade after we had
     just moved when a quiet boy in my class asked
     for a ride home. My mother, new to the city,
got lost, and cross-stitched neighborhoods
     in the fading light because the boy didn't know
     which was his, and he started crying, and my mother

started to cry too, and we drove until the boy saw
　　　a familiar park, and eventually we found it,
　　his house, and his mother was on the lawn
with two officers, and she's crying, too,
　　　and then the drive home after, my mother
　　whispering, *Shit, Shit, Shit,* and wiping her eyes.

NEW YEAR'S EVE

So I'll wash this bowl and spoon
and leave it in the rack by the window to dry.

Maybe this is the one I get right
I think as I carry the fat bag to the dumpster

in the alley. This year I'll buy a pasta machine
and learn to roll cavatelli. I'll quit

wandering the 24-hour shops, letting my fingers
glide along the rows of candy display racks,

the soft gummy worms. There's another dead
squirrel on the steps, its eyes snowed over,

tail rubbed raw of fur. One time, six years ago,
the living room full of friends,

Chris put the Beatles rooftop concert
on the projector. One by one everyone came

in from the yard, left the fire pit to burn by itself.
A cardboard Miller case smoldering over coals.

That moment during "Don't Let Me Down"
when Paul shakes his hips, his eyes out

over the skyline like it just wasn't fun
anymore. Then Alex and Emily on the couch,

him dropping her hand to find a cigarette
outside, away from the noise. I don't

have anyone to call or anywhere to be.
I think I'll go lie down now.

MY CAR GOT TOWED

then the oral surgery: my four bad wisdom
teeth ripped from their beds, stitches and bloodgums,
ketamine and my skin pocked from the needle's poke.

The nurse melted into dentist and I couldn't find
the buttons on my shirt when I woke. In a carport
in Tallahassee I saw the rusted grill and gas can,

the blackened logs in the wet pit, a lone sock
in the drive. Out back by the coop, a hen lifted
her wing over her clutch of chicks, shielded them

from the rain. The miracle of feathers drawing
a single raindrop on course from beak to dirt
while inside we shook like pill bottles. I have a friend

who figured out the password for her roommate's
dating profile. Each week she took his pictures
and photoshopped his face a little bit smaller.

After six weeks his face had shrunk to the size
of a baseball on his neck. Three months and no
dates he finally figured it out, but now he's so used

to his profile he thinks his normal face
is huge. Once after dinner while I poured
Kahlua into my coffee, Keith passed around

his great aunt's journal. We touched
the brown pages and the leather binding,
her magnificent looping script. I translated July 19, 1947,

Met Olli today in the Kempinski Hotel. Poor Uncle Hans
never knew about Olli, and neither did my friend until
I was at the family table and could not stop translating

her affair, the dinner ruined. *Last night with Olli*
he poured two glasses of absinthe, then slowly trickled
water over sugar cubes. Hotel after hotel, night

after night, and everyone in tears but me, reading
that beautiful diary. *The green liquor turned to a sudden*
milky mint, "louche" he called it. The summer I was twelve,

the lake went thick with grasshoppers. The docks, the boatlift,
the small shed where life jackets and fish nets were kept,
all covered in thousands of insects. I rode my bike on the path

through junipers and birch trees, beside bogs where
box turtles lay in the sun. It was a game: which grasshoppers
jumped out of the way, which ones popped under my tires.

JIM & MILT'S BAR-B-Q

The first kitchen I ever worked
    was an Italian restaurant on the panhandle,
  and on my first night the cooks made me
drink a shot of week-old oil from the deep fryer.
    They grabbed my apron and slashed it in half
  with their switchblades, locked me in

the walk-in freezer. Later, as I heaved
    rancid fat into the wax myrtle hedge
  circling the bistro, one of the guys
left a warm can of beer in dirt
    for when I was finished. The girl
  I dated then didn't even own a toothbrush,

believed humans were meant to be
    self-cleaning like a dishwasher, never mind
  the crown on each molar, mouth more
filling than tooth, and there I was,
    Cavity-Free Since '93. Gunnar and Chase
  would come by and ask, *You boys thrivin'?*

and we'd hop the fence at the apartment
    complex and drink rum by the pool.
  Nights sneaking in the fire door
of the Palace Saloon to play pool
    and show nail-polished-forged IDs
  for pitchers of Stroh's, mornings

stumbling two blocks to Jim & Milt's
     for their $2.99 breakfast special: coffee
    eggs, grits, bacon, and toast. An impossible
deal served at brown bucket-seat booths
     coated in a permanent slick of grease,
    the menu board on the far wall losing letters

each day, so that by the time I left it read
     BR AKF ST SP CI L. I hate how bad
    I wish I were back in those sticky-sweet
dumb days. Now it's a winter night eight years
     from there and I watch The Grinch
    and shop for Christmas gifts, my house

fireplace-hot against the moaning wind.
     Jim Carrey fills his mouth with Who-pudding
    until he's sick in the snow. A pop-up
cam girl asks me, *Are you a dirty boy?*
     I mute the TV and whisper, *I was,*
    I was, I was. They carve the roast beast.

DEAR KATE

I admit: that night your dogs were stolen
    I was so liquored that I prayed through

every traffic light and downed sycamore
    until your driveway pulled up. Lucky

those thieves had no guts, dropped
    the collars the second the hounds

bared their gums. When I found you
    on the backsteps smoking a Marlboro,

vodka tonic blurring your eyes, you
    swore then that you were going

to start calling my sponsor. I never found
    your Christmas-light bedroom

safe, I never left a single index card
    love note on your windshield,

and not once did I gobble the cheese board
    you smeared over the ottoman —

my memory is so hole-punched
    I'm not sure what's true. I'm sorry

you found me needle-deep in the kitchen
    while the band played out back,

for that time in bed I gave you a bloody
    nose. It didn't bother me when you took

her hand up your dress behind the pool table.
    I could never be the workhorse muddied

in your field, nosing through rut after rut
    of Sunday gray. Please give my sweater back.

Light paper lanterns in your barn, hope these months
    apart will act as kindling. I was the lip balm

on your nightstand, the shattered porcelain
    doll you glued to the shelf. Once

in a movie theater as I stumbled up
    the loud dark, I saw you move seats.

Light faded to black and the hero wept.
    You turned your head and looked for the door.

I PULL ON WOOL SOCKS
AND JEANS, PACK

a small sack with an apple, a notebook. By the time
the sun turns the clouded sky pink, my fingers are numb
and I'm at Prophet's Rock, looking out over the bare oaks.

Last night around the fire pit I trained my eyes on the flames,
let the gravel lot and shrubs grow dark. I decided then
that I wasn't going to spend the rest of the year in the same

lumpy bed, carrying empty cans to the curb, coughing
in the shower until I feel right again. Just last week
on the drive to Omaha I stopped in Adair, Iowa for gas.

I lifted the nozzle back into its holster and saw fogged
station windows, fifteen faces staring over coffee mugs.
I've passed through three hundred miles of cornfields, driving

until my body grows sore in the vinyl seat, and still
a gas stop in a small town is enough to turn my gut.
All this loneliness is like finding a pond in the woods

and not knowing whether to drink or run. The one time
I pulled on camouflage and slept in the mountains
I was feverish by the second day. In the blind I bugled

until a horny buck appeared and I fired that compound
bow into its flank. For six hours I mapped
blood splatters on fallen leaves until they stopped,

and I stood alone in a clearing, all the trees around worn
ragged where elk had shed their velvet against the trunks.
But no buck. No body with a bright green arrow

between liver and lungs, just blood-matted leaves
and the Montana cold, a fever that refused to break.
This morning as I sit, a clutch of geese falls

from the air into the lake on my right, the slushy water
distorting the treeline. Snow starts, slow at first
but then faster and fatter flakes. A loon calls.

ELEGY WITH GULF COAST HURRICANE & PRINCE

after Larry Levis

It's my final day in town. I should wash the sheets
or make a paste of Ajax & Clorox & scrub the sink

but instead I lie on the couch with the shades drawn,
listen to the wind find cracks in the frame. In the morning

I'll shut the trunk for the long drive to Omaha
to see my arthritic mother for Christmas, but now I roll

over, smoke a roach. I'll leave those sheets dirty, I think. Return
home to a familiar mess. The shed with the washing machine

is frozen shut this time of year & I can't find the screwdriver
to chip the ice in the lock. That time in a bar I pulled a knife

& jimmied the pool table coin slot to make the balls tumble
while outside a hurricane rioted. We had nowhere to go,

couldn't afford to board the windows over & drive farther inland,
besides I hated being landlocked & the bar was open. That night

as Sarah rolled to me in sleep, I pulled my hand away from the sweat
on her back as it dripped from her hair down to the folds between us.

It felt like the disaster trickling through the rotted roof above.
So I sat, stood, & walked to the kitchen to smoke, the low glow

no more than a pilot light floating out from the radiator
to my mouth. One time I picked up a coworker who pointed

to his studio of smashed furniture & broken glass, said only,
Please excuse the mess. A clump of his wife's hair syrup-stuck

to the wall in a dripping red stain. There's no telling what we'll do
in the body's violent want for another. So we waited out

the rainy season. She zipped the bag & left, & all over again
I woke & walked & made the days pass. Kate's hands shake

every morning. She promises it isn't the gin, but just last week
on the furnace-hot hardwood we danced, her breath sick with juniper.

Outside it was so cold that my car wouldn't start & we sat
in those seats for twenty minutes until it finally turned over.

At the hotel we stripped, but our skin shrieked against one another,
so I sat on the bed with a drink & she stood in the shower and shook.

On TV *Purple Rain* was playing & she came out towel-wrapped
& said, *Isn't that the dream? To be fingered on-screen by Prince?*

And I will never forget that bed with her, where once the lights
went out, she turned to me & asked, *What if we end up like this?*

II.

THE RADIO SHOW

Jefferson High airs a classic rock radio station,
    and this morning on the way to the grocery store
  two seniors host the chemistry teacher to thank him
for all he's taught them over the years, and everyone
    is blubbering, the microphone sounding wet
  with snot and tears, every three words punctuated

by a deep, flapping snort, and before you know it, I'm crying
    too, just thinking about Mr. Salton and his beakers,
  the safety goggles. What drama for a can of beans.
Inside the sliding doors they arrange the finest fruit
    at the front, but a watermelon is a hard sell
  when you live alone and don't eat. The iron cart's

back wheel wobbles as I push, the steady *thum-thum*
    thum-thum calming. On the radio, Mr. Salton
  explained why chemistry instead of julienned onions
or giraffes, teeth whitening gel or butchered skirt
    steaks: *I like the way things always carry*
  the ability to change, and I thought, *Wow,*

what horseshit. In my high school choir I knew a boy
    named Preston whose sharp tenor cut cleanly
  over the sour-note boys and girls. He wore
a blue sweatshirt almost daily, his *I'm fucked up*
    sweatshirt, and if that dirty cotton crossed
  the carpet you could expect slurs and pinpoint eyes,

all the symptoms of dope before we knew the drug,
     or how the bags under his eyes were really
     perennial bruises from his father's hands. But man,
could Preston sing. Now he's in prison. Stole
     a taser from an officer and robbed a gas station,
     which is the dumbest way to do it unless you beg

to touch the man you're threatening to kill, which I guess
     is family somedays. I said this to my sister
     and she dropped a toenail into my coffee.
She paints portraits. Her shower collects rings
     of acrylic around the drain. Once in college
     I left the bar before last call, and stumbling

through the back streets to my house a man
     slipped through the bushes, his knife glinting
     in the streetlight, and all he could ask was,
Chuck? My luck, that the mugger shared a cell
     with me in county, my old mistakes saving
     a slash across the gut. I wake each morning

at quarter to five. I put the coffee on, pull meat
     to thaw for my dinner. Pork chops on sale
     today, and I fill my cart. Before they signed off
the air, Mr. Salton said, *I can't wait to see who
     all of you become*, as if he didn't already know.

HEAD-ON

In the suburban basement of seventh grade
   and Nintendos, we spun the empty wine bottle

for Ryan's 13th birthday party, and when I pulled
   away from Sierra she wiped her lips and said,

Really? Oh humiliation, that first kiss
   outed by my clumsy mouth, sweet with

Pixy Stix and grape soda, the neighborhood
   kids teasing me for the next five years,

boy of braces and bad mouth. In late high school
   came the rusted sliding doors on every minivan,

drive-thru taco sauce staining my shirt, the prairie
   grass storm-wet and flooded with grasshoppers.

Days I saved drowning toddlers at the local pool.
   Nights I napped through dinner to careen in the four-

door on gravel backroads, corn stalks whipping
   by the open window, chopped voices from a bonfire

I barreled past. Then I was twenty-one in the basement
   of Poor Paul's Pourhouse spinning the wheel

for my chance at a free pitcher, the HVAC vents
   coated in grease and smoke, while Sam screamed

for a bar rag to wrap the cut on his hand.
   I knew a couple who had a kid: healthy, brown

hair, fat cheeks. One day a blood vessel burst
   in her head. Found dead in her crib

with blood-flooded eyes and purple lips. After
   that he drank too much and she kept a boyfriend

in Fremont. I always had the kind of friends
   I could stay up late with, a case of Hamm's

and some plastic chairs in a yard, cold October
   breeze keeping our coats zipped to the throat.

I blame only myself for the language of fiction
   I mastered to avoid truth. How I discipline

fear to avoid facing anything head-on. One night
   I climbed the waterski jump at Lake Metigoshe

as my friends yelled from the boat below. I paused
   in the July night before leaping. My feet split

the cold green water, then tangled in the long
   weeds that rose from the lake's bed.

THE POSSUM

and it would slink   in the blue light

up the drainpipe   that ribbed   the building

across the wooden   banister protecting

the balcony from below   to rest

on the concrete slab   on summer nights

with raw nose   it would pry

at the potted plants   an ashtray   its hairless tail

brushing the furred   broom left leaning

against the stucco   before pressing

its face   against the glass   sliding door

as if it could smell   or sense me

sitting in there   the whole time

watching the invasion

and no call

to animal control   or complex manager

would provide trap   or bait

so with a church key   I carved

    along the rim   of canned tuna

      careful to trim   the fanged lip

and poured   the juice   onto the patio floor

      knowing odor   alone

    would be bait   enough yet

still I poured   rat poison over

      the shredded meat   and sat

    the tin next to   the puddle of fishjuice

by morning   meat was gone

    wet pawprints   on the nickel floor

and the next night   I waited

     it didn't return

   so I waited   again   the next night

    and the night   after that

   watching through   the sliding door —

all that cruelty   only to catch

     my own face

   in the glass

AN OPEN LETTER TO THE BLOCK EXPLAINING THE MISSHAPEN HEDGE AROUND MY LAWN

First, mind your own damn business.

It's not easy waking each morning and wrestling

these branches back into shape,

especially since the soil beneath is fed

from my own drain, which means lately I've taken

to running the shower and flooding the sink

just to help their growth.

Did I tell you about the cat?

His name is D.B. and he lives in some of the branches.

D.B. standing for "Deadbeat" because he's a lazy little shit

who eats every can of tuna I leave out there

and if I try to talk to him about a little *give and take*

he makes sure to throw up while I'm mid-sentence.

It's rude, and makes it hard to yank the buzz saw awake

to carve the limbs if you know a cat

is hiding among them.

It's like Russian roulette, this guesswork of cat naps.

I'm sorry you all have a neighbor like me,

but do you know how hard this is?

I'm just saying there are worse things.

Pretend it's summer. You're pulling a lawnmower,

relentless heat. Already three blisters have pushed

up through your palms. When the engine gives out

and you hear mewing in a neighboring bush,

act like your own dumb heart isn't immediate.

Act like you don't also fill a bowl with water

and force the church key through a can of Starkist.

DEAR KATE

Do you remember when we went to the zoo?
  I'll never forget your face when that walrus cut you

    in line for snacks. It was never your style
to be so patriotic, yet here you are, flag in one hand,

croquet mallet in the other. I'm just a three-headed
  dog of myth, too much mouth for one gut.

  I'm sorry for the time I left you at the mall.
You survived for three weeks on gumballs and Orange

Juliuses, and when they finally found you
  in the closet of an H&M, you were so feral even the dogs

    hid their tails. I'm sorry I keep changing my story,
that for every dead-end alleyway you find me in

there's a part of the past that chased me down there.
  I sold the lawnmower so there's nothing to be scared of.

    Something big is happening, Kate, and lately the magnitude
has been catching up with me in every gravel lot

and pint night. I've become the last man on earth
  without the vaccine, infected entirely.

Find me at the public park wearing nothing
but cashmere and track pants. Behind the tire swing we can try

to get this back on track. Kate, Kate, we have become
        such anesthesiologists, terrified of the smallest error.

        What do you say? I'll roll up my sleeve and you can
slide the needle in. On the way out the door, stop

in the waiting room and collect my things.
        My bag's the one labeled "Not for Human Consumption,"

        and I know that warning is another you'll test.
Each train of thought a caboose on fire.

BARRICADES

Around the courthouse they've built orange and white barricades,
directed traffic to side streets to stop heads craning from car windows,
and as I walk the dog this morning with Kate, she turns to ask,

What do you think? and I say, *Must be a protest.* When my dad gave
the eulogy at my grandfather's funeral, one woman afterwards
was appalled that he quoted Grandpa's favorite phrase, *Smiling like a cat*

eating shit. In her chapel nothing could be worse than something
that profane, and my dad just smiled and nodded at the open casket
behind him. What a messy world we live in. Just last week I drove

to the state park and brought home a bass to fry for dinner.
After I filleted the smallmouth, I poked through its stomach to see
what bait to use next time, and there among crayfish shells

was a sterling silver wedding band, which tells me two things:
1) After sweating for three hours in Loose Lefty's Tavern,
some poor bastard stood on the river's bank and hurled his ring

at the current where it quickens around a fallen tree,
and 2) Even fish know they can feed on grief, that inside
ordinary suffering there is usually someone who attaches

like a limpet to a sea stone. *Room for Lease* stapled to a barricade,
and Moody does his business by a potted plant behind the halfway
    house.
When we turn the corner to pass the court a second time,

a sign by the marble steps reads *Round the Fountain Art Fair.* One
paint-smattered canvas makes all three of us stop. It shows a dog lying
beside a woman's cot, her head wrapped in bandages, and by the dog's

mismatched eyes you can tell the artist is amateur, but there's something
there, a wanting to organize pain into something useful. It hits all of us.
Even Moody sits down to look, his tail flat on the sidewalk.

ELEGY WITH PARROT & TOM PETTY

Inside a coffee shop I stand beside creamers & straws
& wait for them to call my name. The windows fog over

in the sudden March damp, the common loons crying
from a pond across the boulevard, & when the barista sings

my name, a strange man with a canvas bag takes
the cup & leaves. *This is a coincidence,* I think. *I must*

share his name. That night four years ago Rob got
beaten in the alley behind the bar. We sat on my carpet

drinking cans of Genesee & listening to Tom Petty,
& soon Rob was out on the balcony screaming, *No, I won't*

back down into the rain-wet palms. I knew a woman then
who asked me to be part of her art project, to come

to her house one Saturday night. In her living room
stood a plywood wall she'd painted politicians on

in grotesque caricatures. Lincoln with a mole the size
of a baseball, Nixon with jowls like catcher's mitts,

& at each crotch my friend had carved holes that she asked me
& five other volunteers to stick our penises through,

& though I was Clinton & wanted to play the part, I couldn't
get it up & left. That cavity empty for the shoot, plywood sawed

& painted in a living room with no couch, road that dead-ends
at a dumpster where possums scavenge beneath floodlights.

When the Dundee Theatre closed I attended the final film,
& halfway through *Bridge on the River Kwai* the reel gave out,

lights came on, the audience in red plush chairs stunned
by sudden bright. Sometimes I stand in crowded bars

& look at all the faces, worry they've all secretly gathered.
Everyone who hates Charlie, meet at 8:00, & they stand in their groups

just to exclude me. Or maybe it is me. Every time I've thought
I need to get out of this city, I've moved somewhere else,

but eventually the same quiet malady arrives, the one
that makes me sit in a plastic chair beneath string lights

as the street floods with another spring storm, the window cracked
so the stereo can drift out onto the porch, my legs crossed

& my eyes closed. In a Dallas hotel my nose bled
onto my one good suit, & later in the street a man with a parrot

on his shoulder screamed *Help me! Help me!* as three plainclothes
officers lifted him into the van. That same year I slept on the train

station floor against a duffel bag while Russians peddled porn
in the corner. When I woke, my shoes were gone but nothing

else, & I boarded the intercity barefoot but still okay, the sun's
bloody yolk spilled, clouds covering Earth like bubble wrap.

III.

BIRD'S APHRODISIAC OYSTER SHACK

In downpour-soaked sweatshirts, Jay & I sat at picnic tables in the
   broken-shell
parking lot, chipped paint & plastic pitchers, & devoured dozens of oys-
   ters raw

in their shells, a squirt of hot sauce or squeeze of lemon to cut against
the sun overhead, & both of us, Jay & I, unshaven & brain-fried,

lonely as fence posts, would watch the traffic on Bronough drip past.
Chelsea, server on Sunday afternoons with her always-wet hair

& tattoo sleeves, stood in the doorway of the kitchen with a cigarette,
scrolling on her phone, or squatted against the wall with her head

in her hands. She shifted temperaments like a Gulf Coast storm, swinging
between the simple kindness of joining our table for a beer after her shift

or walking away from us mid-sentence. In my head I can still hear
the shattering of shells as cars pulled in & out of the parking lot, like
   one thousand

broken bottles swept by a push broom across a factory floor. I love beer.
I drink it every day of my life. In Fort Collins, Colorado, I toured the
   Funkwerks

brewery & more than the sugar & yeast musk comes the sound of the
   dumpster

pouring shards into a garbage truck, all that broken glass falling in
 a rapid

wave of greens & browns, the noise clearing each bird from the trees
 overhead.
I'm embarrassed, today, of what my life looked like then: bare mattress

beneath the window, trashcan on the balcony filled with cigarette butts,
wide mirror above the bathroom sink that I stuck post-it notes on,

Do Better. Get oil change. At night I'd sit out on the balcony with the
 door open
behind me, listening to my dad's Neil Young records, the moon an ugly
 man

looking down on me. It's better now. I've got a ribeye dry-aging in my
 fridge
& a fresh can of shaving cream in my bathroom. On weekends I drive up

past the jail & park my car in the trees, walk down the rocks until I'm
 on the bank
of the river. Sandwich packed, two cold cans, a bucket of chicken livers,

I cast my line & sit with a paperback until tension breaks my reading
& I pull a catfish to shore. I lower its body back into the stream, feel

its slick skin against my own as it shudders once, then darts into the reeds.

AFTER FORGETTING TO GO
TO THE GROCERY STORE AND
THE ARGUMENT THAT FOLLOWED

The rain this morning falls
in pockets over the lake,

disturbing the surface like bass
surging for mosquitos. On the far

shore the blackhaw shrubs beat
themselves up in the wind.

The person I love most
is in a diner with coffee and a newspaper,

her ballpoint filling in the crossword.
She watches the kitchen's swinging

door as it strobes glimpses
of the cook and his knife,

the mise-en-place piles of onions
and carrots, a shallot. Before

I could take even one good look
the sushi restaurant downtown closed,

converted to a law office. I think of
those raw fish portioned into boxes

and given to the cooks as part
severance pay. They stand

in their small kitchens and carve
the filets, and when they are done,

they fold poor knives back into
rolling bags, place them in cupboards

beside garbanzos and Tabasco. Late at night
while a *Seinfeld* rerun plays on TBS,

they slide the cold fish
out of the boxes in the fridge, pluck

the yellowtail and bluefin with their fingers,
slowly chew. I adore those now-jobless cooks

with their legs crossed on the ottoman,
one sock just a little loose, peeling slice

after slice of raw fish. I give up
trying to stay dry this morning

and now the rain comes cold on my face.
I walk the shore and scare the catfish

into muddy clouds that bloom
among the reeds. I've forgotten

about the one I love, doodling a dog
on the wet corner of her newspaper.

I care too much for the chefs with
their knives unused in dark apartments.

I wanted only to walk beside the lake
and instead I've been hurtful,

dreaming of scaleless fish and steel
counters where rice was rolled.

I should be there eating toast
and laughing at the dog lifting his leg

in the Business section. Instead I watch
a cormorant fly across the lake,

eyes on the water below.
Back in the diner a waitress

walks the floor with a carafe.
She pauses at the window,

watches the rain for a while,
then lifts a platter for table four —

three plates of raspberry pancakes
and back bacon. Hash browns and eggs.

SELF-PORTRAIT

In the alley behind my house
  a raccoon bloats, rots
    in humid summer, and rather
than pull the shovel
  from the shed and scoop
    the poor guy into a hole,
I watch his decay each
  sad cycle of the sun's heat.
    The slack maw of my apathy
swallows more than I care
  to admit. Bags of fruit
    turn slop in the fridge
door, the slow crust
  ringing the mouth
    of each toothpaste tube.
Each Sunday's slow burn:
  lines cast with bobbers
    and wormed hooks
as I doze on the bank.
  The pole cradled between
    prayer-locked hands.
  Lazy. A turtle in the sun.

DEAR KATE (POEM IN WHICH THE SEINFELD THEME REPEATS ON ENDLESS LOOP)

Giddy up, Kate! Now we'll cross the cobblestone bridge
      in our stream-wet Nikes, and the bars haven't done last call
so we've got places to be! In a vineyard near your hometown

      this would have been called foreplay, but here
you buy round after round to make sure I pass out.
      Look, you really screwed the pooch on this one, kid —

I wake and clean and by noon I'm standing in my office
      with the door locked, dry heaving into a filing cabinet.
I found the salami that can cure any headache,

      and what do you say? You run for hours and don't stop
until your toenails pop off. Stop calling me *friend*. I'd marry
      the deli worker if I could — she wears the same *I don't know*

face of yours. The wind here blows so loud at daybreak
      I can't be heard screaming. I sit next to the lake
shaped like your profile, feeding ducks entire baguettes.

      Your style of journalism consists of uncovering places
without me. Kate, your vanishing act is no means of living.
      Christmas Eve ten years ago you passed out at the table,

and it was so sweet my mother cried. I still cherish that scene:
us all holding hands singing a Whoville *Dahoo dores,*
the tablecloth blooming a pool of drool under your slack lips.

UPHILL DRIFT

I slouch now in a good chair, watching episodes
    of *The Twilight Zone*, the 1950s fears,
loneliness and aliens, and it's so strange
how before we'd been to the moon, TV made
    that rock magnificent. Now I pull
the blinds to keep out its ordinary glow.

I knew a guy in college, Sam, who wouldn't go
    on first dates during a full moon.
Nothing superstitious, just afraid the light
would play across his face and make his acne
    gleam, how one thing becomes another
after a second glance. An alligator lurking

a southern swamp is just a log trolling
    the murky shallows. I will slice
an onion thin enough to see through
but can't comb my hair so it doesn't splay
    like a feral cat. When I was a boy I found
my mother's pink sword in her drawer,

the one that vibrated when turned. Last week
    I went down Gravity Hill in Mooresville, Indiana,
put my car in neutral at the bottom of the slope,
and drifted slowly uphill. The locals swear
    in 1938 a school bus stalled on the train
tracks there, and now the ghosts of dead kids

wait to push your car back up to safety, but truly
　　　the mind's dumb perception is to blame.
　　An ordinary downhill that tricks the eye.
　　　　One time Sam left the house for a date and I teased
　　　　　him for his mousse-slicked hair. Had I known
　　that a car with smashed headlights blending

with the dark would clip him, I would have asked
　　　him to stay a while longer. Last night
　　　in the March cold I walked home from pizza,
a round of darts, and at the intersection on Main
　　　an ambulance waited at the red light.
　　Through the swinging doors I could see

the patient's black mess of hair spilling over
　　　the stretcher cot, until the light changed
　　and there was only a leather bag with clumped tassels.
In the neighbor's yard lay a broken airplane wing.
　　　No, only a snowbank, melting.
　　Letting the light strange its long shape.

POEM WITH A JUGGALO
IN PLAIN SIGHT

It's September and I'm *hot!*
as I stand in front of the shower-wet mirror,
so I think, why not strut myself to the nearest bar?

It's leaf season and that means the mice
have their own little parade down my street
and I make sure to stand to one side to pay my respects.

When the neighborhood girls on their banana seat bikes
come tearing down the hill, I fear for their lives,
those mice. Every year here there's a big festival.

People travel from all over the state and put on their best
Australian accents and see who can do the longest
handstand. When I showed up with jeans on my arms,

legs through a flannel shirt, tennis shoes on my hands,
I fooled all of them. I stood in the street for two hours
and everyone loved me. That is a good memory

of mine, I think. On Sixth and Main, the door
to a Soda Fountain chimes while a little girl sits in her stroller.
Her dad comes out wearing an Insane Clown Posse shirt,

an ice cream cone in each hand. He gives one
to his waiting daughter and she spreads it on her cheeks like face paint.
As if on cue, the breeze stirs up and the sky floods with birds.

NOTE TO THE HOMEOWNERS
FROM THE HOUSESITTER

— for Don Platt

All's well, the cats behave, and your cucumbers are now pickles.
Don't know why I did that, but I came back a little loose

one night and brined everything in sight.
Why I agreed to housesit is beyond me.

I moved to this city two weeks ago and already I'm running
favors, clipping grass, filling hanging petunias with tap water,

all the shit that makes me feel so landlocked here.
I came from the coast but here at night the heat sweats through

your walls as I lie naked in your daughter's bed.
She's in France, so no need to worry. I imagine you let her

into the yard one day to play and she skedaddled
the second you turned your eye. That's a symptom of this house,

the need to bolt. The cats do so twice daily,
a habit that fills my free time standing on the deck,

calling their names. I miss their company, but their absence burns
the day. The other thing I've been doing (forgive me) is polishing

off case after case of Hamm's. Something perverse
in nursing my hangovers in your sober house, cleaning my sick

with your towels stacked by the A.A. meeting schedules,
Morning Meditation highlighted. Let's just say I'm doing everything I can

to not make this move permanent. Let's just say
I struggle to masturbate when every wall is scattered with family portraits.

The one of you four in front of the Lincoln Memorial is especially
judgmental. Last night I crossed the bridge to get sandwich meat,

crossword puzzles, a potato, and on the way back I took a wrong turn
and ended up in your driveway. Is that how you chose this house?

Sweet GPS, show me a porch to fill with wisteria.
I'll admit: in the morning when I crack eggs

into a skillet and fill the room with Van Morrison,
it all makes sense. From the table with my breakfast

I can see into the den, how the sun piles boxes of warmth
on the floor by the windows, Alice and Zoey purring

on the rug. A June sunrise setting the lawn's dew on fire
at your house, as I sit and spill three golden yolks.

SWEAT

July at the insurance office we take
      the elevator to the top floor, all of us
    packed in like so many sides of beef
sweating out, and even the plastic water cooler
      does nothing to stop the heat. Whenever I sweat
    I think of each blast of cold I did not savor:

walk-in coolers in the back of a diner,
      those winters in North Dakota
    when the sun, too lazy to ever fully rise, drifts.
That summer in Florida when I'd go to the Publix
      on Old Bainbridge because they had the best
    A/C. I'd spend whole Sundays pacing

around in my swimsuit, picking up
      and putting down every jar of pesto
    just to feel my shirt cling cold to the wet spot
on my back. The pool at my apartment
      complex by mid-June was completely
    overcome by geckos. This must

have been during the Weed Drought of '13
      when I sat shirtless and smokeless
    on the balcony most afternoons and let sweat's
condensation drip and blend in my bellybutton.
      One night I slipped leaving a cab
    and slammed my finger in the door, went to sleep

numb, but by the time I woke, my finger had grown
      into a throbbing grape. At the doctor's they ran
a flame under a needle and drove the point
straight through the nail, the stream
      of hot blood making a sweet arc into the sink.
I keep thinking that if maybe I could find

one big cucumber to mix with this briny air
      life of mine, I'd feel a little more pickle
about it all. At the top of a Swiss mountain
my brother and I went out into the snow, twenty degrees,
      but because atmosphere thins three miles up
we took off our coats and ate salami in the sun.

BLOOD

Once in Omaha I worked the kitchen line,
and as the boss honed his knife over a tenderloin,
he collapsed. My hands cracked his sternum,

pumping whatever life I could, and he died.
Once at fifteen I came home late, a little drunk
from sitting on the bank of the Missouri, watching

the brown water gush past, and my sister pulled me
into her room. On her bed spread a deep red stain,
and not knowing if it was period or first sex, I took

the rag from her and scrubbed. Our mother would
hand me a shovel on the porch to hold over a snake's
nest to cut heads cleanly from bodies. I think

of St. Januarius, whose blood is preserved in a glass
vial at the Cathedral in Naples, and each year in May
the faithful come to watch it melt from dust back

into blood, and I wonder if each year snakes congregate
on the shed floor under that rusted spade. Once
in an AA meeting a man told us the story of waking

to a warm trickle on his face, his six-year-old son standing
over him with hands bloodied from last night's broken bottles,
I'm sorry, Daddy, I'm sorry, Daddy. The man said,

Sobriety is just like lobster: all claw and shell until
something cracks. I used to love a woman who fainted
if she saw blood, and once I asked her if blood in movies

makes her nauseous, and she said, *A person becomes nauseated,*
not nauseous. Last night I sat in my car in the parking lot
of the Indiana Blood Bank, eating a drive-through

burger. I watched the needle-workers roll out a cart
of biohazard bags. I imagined those bags fat with bad
blood that could help nobody, and I thought of my father,

and his father, too, and my brother whose blood won't
clot. The fluorescent sign flickering in the fog, turning
the droplets on my windshield red as they trickled.

POST-CHRISTMAS

If I have to wash one more dish I'll burn this house down.
Every year it's the same: *You never come home, tell us
what's eating you*, but the answer is always a fat, whiskeyed
grin and shrug. It rained all day and now I'm late for nothing,
so I keep putting on my coat before remembering I don't
smoke anymore and getting wet on Christmas is as evil
as wearing red to school or eating cookies in odd numbers.
The dog said the blessing last night and we couldn't tell
when it ended so our table was a steady murmur of *Amens*
and *Yes sir* until someone finally looked up and stabbed
the roast. I want to be interested in history, but I hate
my own so I can't imagine others being any better,
besides the *past* is just one letter short of being a paste
I can close over these burns with and pretend they're pink.
Tickle me and watch coins fall out. I have collected
so many different ways to pack the car and leave.
When my brother's appendix burst we knew the potatoes
had cooked but would be gummy. Every eggnog,
every wassail. My lover couldn't make it this year —
she got lost on her way and now every lightning flash
is a searchlight. I am garland, I am pine,
I am Christmas-drunk divine are all things I've sung
while watching my father wrestle the tree. Sapped
and bloody, he lectures us on game show rules. I dropped
a drink and now I'm sticky as a porno theater
is something Kate would have said. I miss her,
but Christmas is family and family is forgotten,

or something like that. I'm terrible at quotes and even worse
at dancing. Let me stand on the deck and watch the poplars
drip. A rabbit is running through the grass. I could kill him
so easily is something humans have always thought,
and today is no different. I smell almonds in the kitchen.
Let's take a bite and hope for the worst.

ELEGY WITH SCAT PORN
& MICHAEL JACKSON

When I went down into the woods that first day of winter,
I found a car door against a tree trunk, the paint rubbed thin

from deer shedding their velvet, the pieces of skin dried up
like leather beneath. I have a friend who works wildlife

for the State of Indiana, & she shows me videos of dead deer
they find in the woods, succumbed to a parasitic brain disease,

& the only way to map progress of infection is to carve,
slowly, the skull with an electric saw until the scalp

& scarred antlers tumble to the forest floor, the rotted brain exposed.
In high school there was a custodian, Mike, who bought

pills from the football team until one day they found
him in a bathroom stall, masturbating to a scat porn

magazine, & from then on nobody looked at him, afraid
their own desires would be scrutinized. I always left

the theater mid-movie to sit in the backseat of my car,
that final half hour to myself. Later, I waited in the Children's

Hospital as the neighborhood boy died, & he just repeated,
More morphine, Mom, more, while outside it snowed.

There are still days when I put on Billie Jean & try to moonwalk,
but it's hard seeing Michael's face, knowing what we know now.

There was an entire summer I slept on the floor of my apartment.
I'd leave work at midnight, pass the McDonald's drive-thru,

turn around and get food, & sit on the floor eating burgers, fries.
It made sense to sleep there, but first I stood on the balcony

underneath the palm tree & looked out into the other buildings,
at windows with the lights still on, while inside, behind me,

Elvis Costello played on the stereo, my final summer in Florida
before I had to leave. *My aim is true,* I'd sing along, the window

A/C unit sputtering awake, a lone possum rooting through bags
in the dumpster across the lot. It's snowing now. Outside

my room with wooden floors & tall windows
the ryegrass disappears under the falling flakes.

At my feet a space heater's red coil glows. I want
to always remember that night with my brother

& sister five years ago: we had reservations for hot bowls
of pork belly ramen, but first we went for drinks,

& the whole time the snow was coming down as we sat
in the bar's basement, the heat turned up past comfort,

my feet sweating in my wool socks. By the time we left
the snow had covered everything. Streetlights flashing

yellow. Shopkeepers sliding their iron windows shut. Cabs turning
their lights off one by one. And I trailed behind the two of them,

arm in arm, as they walked forward into the falling snow, the smell
of pork fat & garlic leading the way to the steel noodle counter.

ORIENTATION MATERIAL
FOR A NEW NEIGHBOR
RENTING THE UPSTAIRS UNIT,
513 PERRIN AVE., LAFAYETTE, IN

Don't act so innocent in your Keds and crew neck tee
like some Foreign Agent infiltrating the smallest sect of choir boys
whose a cappella numbers lack depth but bounce just fine.

Meanwhile I sit on the front porch eyeing the U-Haul
and refuse to help on principle of pure spite.
I'm thinking in plurals about it all:

stairs you bumble up, your unloaded lamps,
how we never use groceries, singular,
unless we mean the store,

or maybe some people do pick up their soup tin
and think, *Wow, what a great grocery* —
all this to say you're ridiculous

and I can't wait to fall in love with you.
Maybe you have the same feeling,
though not for me, instead some muscled maniac

in a Range Rover, caressing every pup he sees,
his left hand missing a fingernail,
voice smelling like apples and dish soap.

Earlier this summer before the landlord unfucked
the wiring and gifted your floor electricity, I strung a dumbwaiter
in the walls to send messages on index cards back and forth.

You're welcome, but do mind the sawdust in the hall.
I crave water chestnuts and milk stouts. What do you think
of the Indiana sun? An oozing boil or a fat heirloom tomato?

You'll get used to its nonchalant way of disappearing
for months and returning drunk and furious in May,
cruel as a wound that won't scab. Ever notice

how cuts in the mouth stay open until they close?
That's how this house works: washing machine in the basement
that leaches detergent, front deck that sags in the rain.

Here: as you finish with the truck, let me go inside
and put some music on so loud your packing peanuts vibrate.
A couple of songs about long highways and wet trees,

a slow one about arguments and makeup sex,
and my original composition featuring the garbage disposal.
Are you as excited as I am? Come meet me on the front lawn,

weeping at the sight of your car in the drive. There we can exchange
blows until I'm so bloodied you carry me in your arms
through the front door. Oh, Neighbor. I love you, I love you.

DEAR KATE

— after Josh Bell

i.

You arrived kayak-bound and waterlogged
to the smallest island in Indiana and for three
months you wore nothing but your small-faced

attraction to no one. I smoked more and wore
my loudest shoes so I could be heard coming
around every corner. Did it work? Please respond.

Did you Pavlov my woodclop and nicotine
or is it every burly carpenter that sends you spiraling
into arousal? I've got a hammer on my nightstand.

When I was still an understudy in *Kate, the Musical*
I spent all the money on nachos and watched
you dance at the Sixth Street Dive. Cilantro, lime,

gut rot tequila. Oh sweet, sweet Kate,
you didn't have to tell my brother you hated him.
At the bar in Terra Haute when the drunk called

me *your husband*, you vomited, and whether it was
the thought of us in wedlock or those fried pickles,
the message was clear. It's always snow and then it's not.

I miss you. Open your fingers and I'll give you a handful.
Write down your address, I'll mail you a blizzard.
Once, outside a movie theater I turned to drop

the stub in the trash and you vanished into a cab.
I never meant to be Kate's Ugliest Character Trait.
You, who says, *Go on*, as both command and question,

remember the heated dark of the hotel room
when I turned and made three promises:
one involving a hand and its ring, another in defense

of poppy seed teas, and the last your poor anemic legs,
how they were bruised before we even touched.

ii.

Kate, I'm roasting   an entire bird for you.
        I fucked up   and left the feathers on,
                but you've never   minded

the taste   of flight.
            Make yourself   comfortable.
        I'll get out   the camera

and you can   call me *Zapruder*,
        love   the grainy film
    I take of your head   rolling back
        in my bed.   Is that in poor taste?

You always said   I tasted excellent.

      Kate, I'm sorry   it was your fault,

  but I can   work hard

to make it up.   I wrote thirty novels

   last night   and they all began

      Close the book   now, please.

I'm good   at getting nowhere,   but you knew that.

    Look,   at my mother's house   I blacked out

        your face   from photos

you weren't   even in,   now all that's left

     of Christmas '08   are sharpie stains

and a dried-out wishbone.   Call me thorough,

   but I like my birds   featherless.

    Kate, mate me.   I said *date*

but sex   always sneaks in   past the bouncer

   in my chest.   Kate, you are the drunkest

Zamboni driver   on love's ice rink.   At the birthday

   dinner when we yelled   *Gabi, surprise!*

you grabbed   my crotch   and whispered

      Open your thighs

69

THANKSGIVING

Find me sweating into the sink
        as I peel potatoes. In the other room,

Steve Martin & John Candy share a hotel bed
        while my brother smokes pot in the garage.

I want this goddamned dog to quit yapping
        at my feet, so I look down & see it's *not*

the dog at all, it's my mother & she's on
        the floor, pretending to be a dog begging

for potato scraps. Where is that boy
        who split his skull against the brick fireplace?

That's me, & he's feeding buttered skins
        to his barking mother. I can hear

my sister in the upstairs room, moaning
        to hold music from a collection agency.

Oh, family. What a time to be alive
        is something my dead friend would have said.

I hated his eulogy, but now I can't look
        his mother in the stye. Last week the doctor

told me I was dying. *You have only forty*
            to fifty more years. It's truly liberating,

the way dying forgives my recklessness.
            Sure, I'll have another stout. Make it two.

The trick with the turkey, my dad says,
            is to make sure it's dead. The joke was good

the first time, but twice a day for eight years?
            Even better. Let's fast forward to when

I'm bloated & my lips are covered in bird
            grease. For once the record player skips

the bland tunes & Bill Withers croons.

ALGEBRA OF PLEASURE

Like almond oil over smooth skin I run
   the mop in the hardwood living room,
open all the windows for the cardinal
   songs to flood through. Hot damn I love
the afternoon, a mad wind blowing
   from the Great Lakes, while inside
Jeopardy! plays on TV. Alex Trebek,
   you handsome old thing! I roast pork
until it's tender and toothsome,
   uncork the last good bottle of wine
and wait. Most days being home
   is like playing Monopoly with no dice —

just aimless moving and staying out of jail.
   Once, inside a Whole Foods in Indianapolis
I heard a kid's scream rise over the jars
   of ghee and liquid aminos, *I want coconut!*
She yelled and yelled until I was ashamed
   of my ciabatta and Port Salut, my bottles
of Belgian ale. I turned the corner to see
   her shouting at her stuffed horse,
and I felt true love, for I also ask so much of those
   who can't meet my demands. I challenge
parking attendants when the total comes,
   rage in the post office when the chained pen

is inkless. I know an old German immigrant
  who sings the Oscar Mayer wiener jingle
to herself, mindlessly, all day, simply
  because she loves how purely American
that song sounds. I fail the algebra
  of pleasure that most master daily.
I love the butcher with his coils of sausage,
  steaks stacked in a glass case, but hate
taking a number, so I never go. Instead I'll drool
  the dream of tenderloins and lamb shanks.
Even the buttercream frosting
  on the birthday cake is too sweet

and grits on my tongue. I pull the space heater
  out from the cellar and plug it in the slow-drying
room while outside I wring the mop into shrubs.
  Next door my neighbor has his truck up on blocks
and the hood popped. Some '80s hair band
  belts from his stereo, and though I can't make
out who it is, I hear the frontman in his leather pants
  and face makeup, a Mötley Crüe-type glam
that shoves my face into a dumb grin.
  My neighbor waves at me on my porch,
so I nod the soggy mop back, like some
  wet and wild headbanger in a crowd.

TABLE SCRATCH

Last dollop of sun sinking, flooding
    floor-to-ceiling windows
        where I rack fifteen polished
balls, chalk the cue. Here, beer is poured
        either in freezer-frosted mugs
    or not at all. The only place

this side of the river with tables,
    I must suffer
        bartenders who blare
metal and refuse to swap dollars for quarters,
        though I love the tattoos
    splayed across their throats.

I imagine the intense
    pain of the ink gun
        on an Adam's apple,
teeth clenched,
        skin raw for days.
    At each table, pairs

and threesomes connect
    one ball with another, chain
        reaction complete with swears
and knuckle-brushing,
        one fist against another.
    I choose a table beside

the windows, tinted
     so strangers can't gawk
         as I swap cues
off the rack on the wall.
        Across the street a woman
     scoops birdseed from the trunk

of her car and scatters it
     across the plaza, finches
         flocking stubbled cement.
In a far corner, one girl sinks the eight so another
         in black leather pulls
     her for a kiss.

A single strike separates
     one ball from another. They say if Earth
         were this size,
it would be smoother than the white
         cue I place to break.
     My own stick slips,

sending a yellow and white stripe
     over the table's lip
         to the carpeted floor.
A deadened thud, and no one
         turns to look as I scoop
     the ball back to the table.

Beer fills a frosted mug.
     I chalk the cue's tip. Then break —
         a shattering scatter, like turning

the crank on a grocery store candy machine,
            countless jellybeans rushing
        into my open and cupped hand.

LEAVING LAFAYETTE

And I'll bet for a nickel that behind
  Menard's I could still find our pond
    where the long grass is matted flat.
      How we used to go sit with fishing gear
        and cold beers those June mornings.

Over at the brewery where the car
  died, we just stayed until closing,
    eating bar pretzels and watching folks
      speed down 9th on their way home.

That studio apartment where I first lived,
  remember it? You found it charming
    how the sink and shower ran at the same
      time, even just trying to wet a toothbrush
        or rinse blood from a hangnail's mess.

That Saturday we drove a half hour
  to Delphi just to see the robot opera,
    those costumes of aluminum foil tubing
      and spray-painted jeans, we laughed

so hard in the theatre the flashlight
  came on. That one actor knew none
    of his lines and couldn't dance worth a damn,
      but god we loved that show. Arm in arm
        afterwards we wanted to go for a drink,

but every shop window had posters
  for the two girls who disappeared
    by the river, ten grand reward
      for finding the man responsible.

Look, if you have to go to New Zealand,
  just go. I can stick around here a while
    longer, with the wood steps I slept on the night
      my key broke in its lock. Long painted
        brick walls we stood against in the rain

trying to get cigarettes lit. I could gather
  every last bit of it just to prove a point:
    none of this will change unless
      you stay. Just look at that truck

with antlers on the grille, the dust
  it kicks up as it spins out of the lot.
    Overhead, clouds drift and separate,
      like shelves of ice that break
        from shore to float downriver.

ELEGY WITH ROTTING PUMPKIN
& MICK JAGGER

Those final years before I left Nebraska, my mother spent
all day sleeping in a green armchair, or standing on the wood

deck, looking out over the retreating treeline, scanning
for a cardinal, a possum. The swaying figure of my father came

& went as he pleased, & I felt then that something was wrong,
something I wouldn't come to know until years later

when I lived alone for the first time. Afternoons
I sat & wrapped twine around the pink legs of a bird so

they wouldn't splay in the oven's heat. It made sense then
never to come home. That winter I stood naked

over the iron grates on the floor as the heat blew & watched
the snow cover the steps leading to the wood slats

of my front porch. Sometimes there's nothing I can do
to stop myself from hating the man in the auto parts store

who doubts I can change a headlight on my own,
then I hate him more when I walk back from the rain

to ask for his help. I used to go to parties at night,
have my drinks, talk to people. After I walked home alone

I'd watch the Rolling Stones play their sold-out show
in Tempe, Arizona, 1981. Before the first chord hits,

Mick Jagger points out & asks, *Are you feelin' goooooood?*
& I'd stand in my living room, wearing only my socks,

& try to imitate his hips & his lips, singing along, *Well ain't I*
tough enough, come on baby please. The morning would show

& I would wake & work the kitchen. At the woodfire oven
in the forest of the Florida panhandle, now & then I'd lose

a blob of cheese from a lasagna pan, & as it hit the oven's stone
floor, I smelled first the melt, then the char. I wander house

to house, room to room, looking in the desk drawers
of strangers, each medicine cabinet a little different from any

other, that quiet noise a doorknob makes when the lock is set.
In a small room my grandfather commanded glass to shape

& soldered together lollipop reds & jay blues, the stained shards
becoming finch or monarch butterfly, the desk lamp

covered with a canvas sheet to simulate the sun's soft light
playing on each suncatcher strung with fishing line from the exposed

wooden beams. Nine blocks from his home I worked
at the Pepsi bottling plant in summers during high school,

the warehouse floor sticking to shoes with each step, & my hands
in those days smelling always like syrup. When my grandfather

died, my grandmother closed that workshop door
& never opened it again. Twelve years later, after the flood,

the hinges swung open to a room of broken glass.
The buffalo grass already turned brown in the cold,

another dark sky moving across that North Dakota town.
On my porch a pumpkin rots, its dull ochre echoing

that Christmas sky ten years ago when I walked the white
street home, each footprint behind me filling in. It's past

eleven & I should be asleep, but on the stove is a pot of apples
& oranges, cinnamon sticks & star anise.

WORLD'S LARGEST BALL OF PAINT

When Jay calls and tells me he's sober, I say,
     Good for you, though in my sauté pan of pity
     for his life and his liquor-slips, I taste nothing.
I hang up and sit on the deck, first hot day
     of spring, the stupid fox squirrels getting laid
     in the trees, squeaking and thrusting against

each other. I'm rarely happy for anyone.
     Each time I hear a beautiful voice I loathe
     the cords in my own throat, their clumsy
vibrations souring each note, so I drift into karaoke
     nights at the local dives, and feel less
     alone in my own bad song. In 1978 my mother

was kicked out of her church choir, she was so flat,
     a fact she loves to mention to this day, bragging
     those howling hymns. That same year she drove
her Volkswagen bug through the North Dakota
     night to a cabin on the Canadian border,
     whipping through birch trees and juneberry bushes,

chorus of cicadas. She fell asleep at the wheel
     and rolled her car six times. As a boy I pressed
     the scars on her legs where she no longer has
feeling, the nerve endings burned out beneath the skin.
     I was once asked to cook spaghetti for 400 people.
     In those days I drove around so dope-loaded my path

was more rumble strip than road. I worked as a cook
        in a ten-table Italian restaurant, and after the head chef's
    dog died, we dug a hole between shed and swamp
and lowered that furred mess. Later, the knife slipped
        and the tip of my finger landed among diced onions.
    The nurse rubbed the nub and bone-studded end

with alcohol and stitched my hand closed.
        I still feel nothing there, middle-finger,
    left hand, maybe as punishment for those numb
years I lived. The gas station down the street has the best
        fried chicken in town. Most nights walking home
    I pop in for a fried tender, the batter forming a crust

under the heat lamps, golden layer sauce clings to.
        Sitting on the curb under that fluorescent sign
    I love to watch the cars at stop lights, music and smoke
pouring out of windows. Red clouds of brake-light exhaust.
        Thursday I drove with Kate to a potshot,
    no-inn town to marvel at *The World's Largest Ball of Paint*.

In the shed behind a farmhouse it hung: baseball
        that's been dipped and smeared so many times
    it now weighs two tons. Visitors fly from all over the world
for the chance to paint on a fresh coat and become the next
        World Record Holder until another tour group
    comes along. Even laughter is its own species

of grief. The couple who owns the ball told us they add one
        layer every single day, a different color than the last,
    so the cross-section of this thing must be a gigantic jawbreaker.

Kate and I smoothed rollers over the ball until the coat
        dried. The owners told us, *That's a World Record!* Dumb,
    gripping the still-wet tools, we watched that paintball swing.

World's Largest Ball of Paint

This Certifies That

Charles Nutter Peck

Has Painted the World's Largest Ball of Paint

Coat # 25387

Color yellow

Date 1-21-17

Signature *Mike Carmichael*

765-724-4088
WorldsLargestBOP@yahoo.com
www.ballofpaint.freehosting.net
Mike & Glenda Carmichael
10696 N 200 W, Alexandria, IN 46001

ACKNOWLEDGMENTS

Thank you to the following journals for first publishing poems from this collection, often in a different form:

Baltimore Review: "Bird's Aphrodisiac Oyster Shack"

Bellevue Literary Review: "Note to the Homeowners from the House-sitter"

Booth: "The Peanut Barrel," "The Radio Show"

Cincinnati Review: "Elegy with Rotting Pumpkin & Mick Jagger"

Columbia Poetry Review: "Leaving Lafayette"

Harpur Palate: "World's Largest Ball of Paint"

The Journal: "Sweat"

Massachusetts Review: "Barricades"

Ninth Letter: "A Small Sweetness," "Elegy with Gulf Coast Hurricane & Prince" (as "From the Smallest Couch in Indiana"), "Post-Christmas"

North American Review: "Elegy with Scat Porn & Michael Jackson"

Poetry Northwest: "Uphill Drift"

Puerto del Sol: "Thanksgiving" and "Orientation Material for a New Neighbor Renting the Upstairs Unit, 513 Perrin Ave., Lafayette, IN"

Quarterly West: "Noise"

Spoon River Poetry Review: "Dear Kate [I admit]" and "Dear Kate [Do you remember]"

Superstition Review: "Head-On"

Tampa Review: "Blood"

Zone 3: "My Car Got Towed"

The poem "Noise," originally published in *Quarterly West*, was selected by Cate Marvin for the *Best New Poets 2019* anthology.

Special thanks are made to Don Platt, whose mentorship, care, and guidance was incredibly formative in the writing of these poems. Every phone call, picnic table meeting, cramped office visit, every conversation shaped this book in some way, and I am grateful for all your support.

Enormous thanks to Kelsey Carmody Wort for your relentless friendship, insight, and encouragement. This book never would have happened without your help. Thanks Kels.

Thanks are also due to the many friends, peers, and mentors who challenged me and offered thoughtful input on early versions of these poems: Marianne Boruch, Kaveh Akbar, Adrian Matejka, Dana Roeser, Diana Clarke, John Milas, Hannah Dellabella, Mitchell Jacobs, and the entire creative writing communities in Lafayette and Tallahassee. Thank you all for your help along the way.

"Elegy with Parrot & Tom Petty" borrows an image from James Kimbrell and thanks him for his mentorship.

To the editorial team at Black Lawrence Press, especially Diane Goettel, for believing in this manuscript and giving it a home.

Finally, thank you to my siblings Alex, Hannah, and Jenna, and my parents Nancy and Dave, for supporting me always, especially when it was difficult. Love you.

©Elisabeth Bay

CHARLIE PECK grew up in Omaha, Nebraska and received his MFA from Purdue University. His poetry has appeared previously in *Cincinnati Review*, *Ninth Letter*, *The Journal*, and *Best New Poets* 2019, among others. His first collection, *World's Largest Ball of Paint* (2024), received the 2022 St. Lawrence Book Award from Black Lawrence Press.